Interview in English

Get your Dream Job in the English-Speaking Workplace

James Levin

© James Levin 2020

All rights reserved.

No part of this book may be reproduced, or stored in a retrieval system, or transmitted in any form or by any means, electronic, mechanical, photocopying, recording, or otherwise, without express written permission of the publisher.

Certain names in this book have been changed to protect the privacy of individuals in the stories. All interviews conducted by author unless otherwise noted. Company names used in examples are fictitious.

Cover design by: Adriano Piccirillo

Table of Contents

Introduction
About this book
Keys to a successful interview

Part I: Before Your Interview
    The right way to prepare
    Order matters
    Common mistakes to avoid in your interview
    The importance of telling stories
    Doing your research
    About your interviewer

Part II: The Interview
    Introducing yourself
    Talking about your experience
    Showing that you did your research
    Thinking forward
    Talking about your strengths and weaknesses
    Tell me about a time ... questions
    It's your turn! Asking your interviewer questions
    Answering a question when you don't know the answer

Part III: After the Interview
    Sending follow-up emails
    Accepting or rejecting a job offer
    Rejection: Recognizing things out of your control
    Why you should act now

Glossary of terms
About the Author

Introduction

Hello, and congratulations. You picked up a book written in English. As a professional communications coach for non-native English speakers, I know how difficult it is to take that step. You're now holding a book written especially for you.

If you think of yourself as an English learner, this book is not for you. You are not learning English; you speak English. It might not be perfect English—no one speaks perfectly—but you can communicate and work in English.

You're reading this book because you want to advance in your career in an English-speaking environment. You are ready to take the next leap in your professional life and move to a position where you will need English every day. That's where I come in.

My name is James, and I have been coaching non-native English speakers like you for the last four years. I have helped people from all over the world find the confidence to start working in their dream jobs, where they communicate in English every day. My clients work in multinational companies like Amazon, IBM, Netflix, JPMorgan Chase, Korn Ferry and others.

They work in these positions because they decided to commit to using English every day and strengthening their communication skills. I was there to facilitate their journey.

You're now ready to take the next step in your career.

About this book

Cathy had a problem.

She had just finished her master's degree in New York and had been interning as a social worker at a community center helping young children navigate social life in a multicultural city.

She liked what she did, and she was good at it. Her colleagues respected her, and her clients were grateful for the work she did.

Now, armed with her master's degree and some hands-on experience, she was ready to apply for a full-time position at the community center. She sent her application and prepared to be called for the interview. She got the call promptly, and the interview was scheduled for the following week.

That's when she started to panic.

Cathy came to the United States from China to get her master's degree. She came with an advanced level of English, and her two years of study resulted in her speaking with a near-native level. Cathy is bilingual and commands her native and second languages well.

But despite using English regularly, she never felt she was able to express herself perfectly. There was always something missing or something stopping her from speaking with the same confidence she could in her native language. And now, she had an interview in a week and her future depended on her ability to express her value using English.

Cathy isn't alone. She's one of the thousands of non-native English speakers who are qualified, dedicated workers but experience a lack of confidence when using their second language. Even though these people have the ability, this lack of confidence is an obstacle that prevents them from getting the jobs they deserve.

Fortunately for Cathy, she found me, and I coached her for the week before her interview. We identified the mental blocks that made English difficult for her and practiced intensively.

Cathy is now a full-time social worker at the company and tells me that it is her "dream job."

Now, for every Cathy, there are three others who don't prepare for their interview and get turned down. Even worse, there are 10 others who don't apply for their dream job because they lack the confidence to work and communicate in English. This book is made for those who need to build the confidence to interview in English.

This is a guide made for non-native English speakers who want to work with English-speaking companies around the world. After reading this book, you will have a clear idea of how to answer the most common interview questions in English and how to prepare yourself for any question you may encounter during your interview.

This book will include examples and useful phrases to help you prepare for your interview. Most importantly, it will show you actionable strategies for your English-language interview. If you're ready to get serious about working in an English-speaking company, this is the book for you.

Of course, learning strategies and useful expressions are only the beginning. As you know, reading about a technique and applying that technique are two very different things. Much like learning a language in school and then speaking that language in another country.

Therefore, to get the most out of this book, I strongly encourage you to speak your answer after reading each section. Even better, record your voice on your phone or another device and listen to yourself speaking later. At the end of the book, I encourage you to contact me and tell me about your experience.

Keys to a successful interview

You've probably already searched online for the most important things to do in your interview. I'm not going to repeat the advice that you've already found. You know it's important to dress well and look the interviewer in the eyes.

This is good advice, but it's not what you need to hear. These are the tricks you learned in first grade, and a nice suit and a firm handshake never earned someone a job by themselves. No advice about body language and eye contact will get you the job. What you really need to know is what to say and how to deliver your message.

In this section, you will learn the keys to a successful interview concerning the language you want to use to make the best impression. Because, at the end of the day, it's not your appearance that will get you the job. It's your ability to communicate your value clearly and confidently.

Starting in this section and throughout this book, you will learn how to use English to impress your interviewer and make yourself an irresistible candidate.

Your interview is not about you

Your interview is not actually about you. But what does that mean? Of course my interview is about me, right?

It's true that you go to interviews to talk about yourself. But to unlock the secret to giving a strong interview, there is another, much more important, question that you must ask.

Why is the company interviewing me?

It's important to flip your perspective. Don't think about how you see yourself and what the job can offer to you. Think about what you can offer the company.

The interviewer is always looking for the people who will help the company grow and thrive. It's their job to find those people who will advance the company, and therefore that's how you must present yourself. You're the person for the job because you will offer the company the most value.

You may want the job because it will look good on your CV or resume, or because it offers a good salary and flexible hours. But that's not what's important for the company, the company offers these perks to attract the most talented people in the field.

Show them why this is you!

Remember this, and suddenly the language you use becomes a lot more conscious. You will make a stronger impression and let the interviewer know that you understand why you are in the room with them. Let's look at some examples.

Instead of, "I want to rise to a managerial position, so I can develop my leadership skills," you say, "I want to become a manager because I believe I have the skills to expand the company's growth."

"I want to take advantage of professional development workshops to become a better worker" becomes "I will continue my professional development, so I can offer more productivity to my bosses and the business."

It's a subtle difference, but it's one that goes a long way. The candidates who understand that their interview is about the company, not themselves, are the ones who will be irresistible to employers.

You are not being judged for your English ability

The most common thing I hear when I begin working with a new client is something like, "I feel like I can't express myself properly in English."

I continue to ask questions to get to know my client and learn about their professional background and job aspirations. By the end of our conversation, the client usually tells me their entire professional background and skills they possess.

And nine out of ten times they express themselves perfectly clearly! I don't mean they speak perfect English. There is no such thing as perfect English. What matters is that the person you're speaking with can understand you and that you can hold a conversation with them.

The problem is not your English ability; it's your confidence to express yourself in English.

When you're nervous about perfect speaking in English, it is easy to think about every little mistake and become flustered in the interview.

It's also easy when you are practicing to focus on your grammar and structure without thinking as much about the content of your answers.

But you aren't competing to be the best English speaker that interviews for the position. You are competing to be the best at doing the job that you are applying for.

We will talk more about how to overcome your fear a lot in this book. In the meantime, when you are preparing for your interview, remember to focus on what you will say instead of how you say it. Creating a strong plan will help you prepare and stay on your message.

An interview is a conversation

When we practice for interviews, it's normal to get so caught up in what we will say that we forget to think about what the interviewer(s) will say. Or worse, we start to imagine their responses.

We think, "Well, I will say this, and then they will ask that ..." and on it goes. We create entire conversations in our heads. Does this sound familiar?

Interviews do not follow a script.

How you react and interact in an interview is just as important as how you answer the questions. Interviewers are looking for someone who will make a good team member. Your ability to show your personality in the interview will be crucial in the decision to hire you.

Of course, the interviewer also has a responsibility to create a conversation. Most interviewers will want to find a natural environment where you can express yourself.

Making sure you are having a conversation is crucial to a good interview. Don't forget, in the interview stage, the company is starting to look for a human being who can work in their team effectively. Be natural, and don't stress over small errors.

Later, we will talk about how the way you prepare for your interview will help or hurt your performance. You will learn about the critical mistakes that candidates make while preparing and how to prepare the right way instead.

You must express your interest in the job

In any language, candidates often leave an interview without properly expressing their interest in the position. This is frustrating for interviewers who are left with an unclear impression.

Candidates, in turn, are so worried about saying the "right" things they leave out the simple statements that will tell the interviewer they want to work there.

Expressing interest can be obvious. For example, you should always say clearly that you want to work at the company at least once during the interview. However, it's also something you can express in other ways.

Asking good questions, connecting your values to the company's and showing that you took the time to research the business are all important ways to show your interest. Later, you will learn how to do this clearly and naturally.

Following these tips as you prepare for your interview will help you build confidence. Keep this in mind as you continue reading and planning your message. With each new question you read about, think about why the company is asking this question. What do they want to learn about you? Remember to focus on what you are going to say instead of worrying about perfect English. Keep in mind that you will be faced with unexpected questions and situations and you must be ready. And finally, think about how you will show your interest.

Interviewers want you to do well

Here's some good news for non-native job applicants. Recruiters and interviewers want you to succeed! In any interview you have, a good interviewer will do everything they can to make you feel comfortable and get to know you.

For this book, I spoke to many recruiters and hiring managers and almost everyone told me the same thing. If you are invited to an in-person interview, they want to hire you. Interviewing takes time and resources for the company, which is why they only invite the best candidates to an interview at all.

If you were called first by a recruiter and they passed you on to their client, you've already passed the hardest part in terms of your English. The recruiter has evaluated your language skills and decided you speak well enough to move on. If you didn't, they will usually tell you.

If you applied for the job and are interviewing for the first time with the company directly, you have a little more responsibility to show your language ability. Still, you're in the room because the hiring staff liked your resume and want to believe you are capable of doing the job.

Recruiters especially want to see you succeed because their

success and yours are related. Vanessa Reis, senior people coordinator at Rise Ventures in Brazil, told me what she does when she has a great candidate but some concerns about their language.

> "That's kind of the action I took when I had this space for people who also were not native speakers, doing an intensive course, let's reevaluate you in one to three weeks. It depends on how urgent the opening is. And then let's talk again and see what we can do. And then in parallel, obviously you or I would go looking for plan B, C, D. So that's how I would do there. But I try to make sure that the person would at least get a shot at doing the job well."

Even if you're not ready to work in an English-speaking environment, it never hurts to keep in contact with recruiters. If you have the qualifications, they will be thrilled to hear from you when you've improved your language skills and you're ready to try again.

> "I usually tell them that they can call me when they feel that their English has improved, and we can see if there is something. I will be able to reconnect with them. And I will honestly do that, and I will be happy to talk to them again." says Renata Horvath, Recruitment Business Partner at Smart Hire Recruitment Limited.

Part I: Before Your Interview

The right way to prepare

If I think back to my first real interview, I don't like what I remember. I spent a lot of time preparing, and I thought I was sure I would get the job.

I had experience, I had researched about the company and I was eager. How could any company resist me?

I put on my best suit, which hung loosely over my lanky frame and emphasized my youth and arrived hilariously early. So early that I forced myself to wait in a park nearby for almost 20 minutes before even going into the building.

I finally got into the room with the interviewer and prepared to impress her.

The interview lasted five minutes. It took just five minutes for her to see I wasn't ready for this opportunity. Here's a word of advice: If your interview only lasts a few minutes, it probably didn't go very well.

A few things went wrong. First, I was selfish. I thought mostly about myself and my career instead of the company. I did my research, but what I learned was superficial. We will come back to doing strong research soon. But the biggest problem was that I prepared in exactly the wrong way. This became clear to me in the first minute and to my interviewer not long after.

Before your interview, you will want to prepare. A lot. Think about the hours you spend studying for tests in high school and university. You would never go into a test without a good amount of preparation, right?

But an interview is not like a test. You might get a second opportunity to take the test. Individual tests do not determine what you will be doing for the next several years of your life.

Now that I've made you more nervous, let's talk about how

you will prepare for your interview.

Each interview question has an unlimited number of possible answers. This is a huge difference between the tests you took in school and the interviews you will do in your professional life. This means that you cannot memorize your answers for the interview like you would a test.

Unfortunately, creating and memorizing exact answers is a natural tendency that almost everyone has when preparing for an interview.

But it's crucial to avoid rehearsing like this, because when you are repeating memorized answers, here's what will happen.

First, it will be difficult for you to listen to your interviewer. If you know what you're going to say already, you will be waiting for the questions you expect instead of listening to what they really say. It's true that several interview questions are predictable, but all interviews will contain variation. This is especially true in today's marketplace. As young, innovative companies dominate the market, their hiring practices and interview techniques can also be innovative and different.

As a result of not listening closely to your interviewer, you may give an answer that you prepared but that is not suitable for the question. This will either confuse the interviewer and leave a bad impression or cause them to ask follow-up questions. Either way, it will be a frustrating experience for both parties and interrupt the natural flow of the interview that you want.

Second, when you rehearse, it becomes more difficult to improvise. Think about the situation above where the interviewer asks you a follow-up question. Of course, you could not have prepared for this second question and you will find it more difficult to answer.

If you are only repeating answers you've practiced before, you won't be ready when a new question comes your way. What's more, when you are caught unprepared, you are more likely to make speaking mistakes which can lead you to become flustered and make more errors.

Finally, if you rehearse your answers, you will sound rehearsed. Unless you're an accomplished actor, a rehearsed answer will always sound different than a non-rehearsed answer. And to almost any native speaker, the difference between a rehearsed answer and a spontaneous answer is painfully obvious. This difference will become even clearer when you answer a question that you didn't rehearse. You may sound robotic and uninterested and will leave an underwhelming impression.

Your objective in an interview is to sound natural and create a conversation with your interviewer that flows easily. You want to connect with them and let them see your human side, not only your professional facade. Rehearsing your answers exactly will interrupt this flow and slow down the interview.

Thinking back to the interview I talked about, all of these issues came up almost immediately. I was ready for the first question: the obligatory "tell me about yourself." I answered as anyone who has frequently rehearsed does—like a robot. It was the second question where things really started to go wrong. It was a question I hadn't prepared for and I failed to impress with my quickly improvised answer. At that point, I was already lost. The following brief minutes were painful. I was mercifully allowed to leave not long after.

If I could go back, I have no doubt I would last more than five minutes. In fact, I now feel prepared to go into almost any job interview and leave a good impression. So now, let's talk about how to prepare correctly and be able to walk into the room with confidence.

There is a correct way to prepare that will help you take on almost any question and create that natural conversation that you are looking for. Think about a math test you've taken. Instead of memorizing answers, you instead would memorize formulas and apply them to different questions.

Interviews are not so different. If you try to memorize your exact answer, you will fail. But, if you memorize the formulas for different questions, you will be adaptable and prepared.

You also want to focus on memorizing talking points instead of every word. What do you want your interviewer to know about you before the end of the interview? What are the themes that you will reinforce throughout the interview?

Let's look at an example. One common question in any interview is, "Why should we hire you?"

Instead of memorizing your answer word for word, create an outline with your talking points. Here, I will provide you with one possible formula. Don't just read the next part. Think about how you would answer using this formula.

"I think you should hire me because ..."

- Characteristic #1 (i.e. "I am a hard worker...)
    - Support
    - Example

- Characteristic #2 (i.e. I am a strong communicator)
    - Support
    - Example

Fill in your formula with key phrases to support your qualities and choose a few words that will help you remember an example. This could be from a specific project or customer interaction.

And that's it! You don't need to write out every word you want to say. You will never remember everything, and you don't want to sound rehearsed. Have a plan, but keep it flexible and focus on the main points with some examples ready to go. Don't worry about memorizing phrases and vocabulary. You're talking about yourself, so you're the expert! Think about what you want to say, not how you want to say it.

As part of my research for this book, I spoke to several hiring experts about the interview process and what they have noticed in their experience.

Renata Horvath, from Smart Hire Recruitment, told me the importance of being prepared. But that doesn't mean memorizing every single word.

"Well, the problem is that when they are under pressure, they will fail to remember. So, I would say instead of a full script, I would say let's have a bullet point of what I'm going to talk about." She says.

Renata was not the only one to mention the pressure of being in the actual interview. Maybe you practiced the perfect answer in your home or with a friend, but when you arrive at the interview, the situation will be different.

Vanessa Reis, who helps companies with recruitment, training and development, said, "Normally, [when a candidate rehearses] they keep searching for that word that they practice or they're kind of nervous because if they forget something, they will probably not get the right message across."

For Vincent Ramos, a Bilingual Talent Acquisition expert at Staples Business Advantage in Canada, the difference between a practiced answer and a rehearsed answer is often very obvious. He says:

"When you rehearse, you start overthinking too much. And then you start thinking and talking like a machine. I remember, I noticed it a lot because when I started recruiting, I needed to learn a lot of things by heart. My question didn't seem natural because those were not my words. They were the words from the sheet of paper. And it shows when you come in like this. So it makes a big difference when they do that. It might come out as close-minded, slow."

Preparing the right way for your interview, and avoiding rehearsing your answers, will help you to feel confident and comfortable once you're in the room. Use outlines and key points when you prepare your answers. Trust in your ability to communicate to fill in the rest.

Order matters

I got my degree in journalism. I spent years interviewing people for stories and helping them feel comfortable speaking about themselves and their accomplishments.

As a journalist, my job was to get the best information out of my sources, and sometimes information they didn't want to share.

When we find the most important information, we put it at the beginning of the article. We call this the "lede."

One of the first principles you learn in journalism school is, "Don't bury the lede."

If the story is about a man who discovered the cure for cancer, you don't start by explaining where the man grew up and who his parents were.

You say immediately, "this is Dr. John Smith and he found a cure for cancer." The most important information goes first. Always.

Even in obituaries, the order is determined by the importance of the information, not the chronological information. For example, look at one obituary of Whitney Houston. The first paragraph talks about "the multimillion-selling singer who emerged in the 1980s as one of her generation's greatest R & B voices.[1]" It does not talk about "the teenager who sang in her church choir" until much later.

Why? Because her international fame is much more notable than her time as a church singer.

In a job interview, you choose the best parts of your experience to share and you decide what is important. When you introduce yourself, you will not start with the job you had in high school restocking supermarket shelves or serving coffee. When you talk about your past experience, you must choose the most relevant information, not necessarily the most recent.

It's especially tempting when you start to talk about yourself to use chronological order. I can no longer count the number of clients who begin to answer that first question with, "Well, I graduated in 2011 with a degree in business management" despite that being almost 10 years ago! When you are introducing yourself, put the most important information first. When you're talking about your skills, put the most relevant ones first. And when you're sharing your goals, put the most ambitious goals first.

Keep this in mind as we start to talk about how to answer different types of questions. Whatever the question is, don't bury the lede.

Common mistakes to avoid in your interview

Again, you've probably already done a web search for what not to do in an interview, and you've found some great advice. In this section, we will talk about the less obvious mistakes that you might make as a non-native speaker. Remember, this book is written for you. These mistakes are the ones I've repeatedly noticed over years of experience and hundreds of coaching calls with clients like you.

You are apologizing too much

First, you're apologizing for your English level. Maybe this isn't you specifically, but there are countless interviewees out there that have the urge to apologize after a small mistake.

Remember that language skills and communication skills are two different abilities. Language is a hard skill, something that you can measure. But it's your ability to communicate, not just your language level, which many companies prize these days.

Vanessa from Rise Ventures says "I think that the language is a technical skill. You can teach much easier the language skill than a behavior or making a connection magically happen. So, I prefer to not judge it as one of the first things that determines if the person is going to get a job."

If you are guilty of apologizing when you say something incorrect in English, I understand. It's a natural reaction after noticing an error or pausing for a little too long while you search for the right word.

You smile and say, "I'm sorry, my English is not so good."

You should not do this.

You must avoid this temptation because you are not there to

be judged for your English-speaking ability. This is not an English assessment test. You are there to determine your ability to do the job the company needs you to do. Your interviewer will not be afraid to ask for clarification if they do not understand something you say.

As for your errors, everyone makes mistakes. What is important is how you react and move on from these moments. Say "excuse me," and continue speaking naturally and calmly. If you apologize, you are showing your own insecurity and undermining your abilities. You would not be in the room if the interviewer did not think you were capable of working there.

If English is a big part of the job, talk about how you are improving your speaking abilities by giving clear examples.

Avoiding this may take some practice. You have to fight the urge to apologize, especially if you have this habit already. When you are practicing your interview with friends or coaches, get used to overcoming small mistakes and continuing. The more you practice, the more confident and prepared you will feel.

Petteri Nakamura, an ICT Service Manager working in Finland, talked to me about the hiring process in his company for this book. A non-native English speaker himself, he talked about the challenges of finding someone who can connect with his team.

Describing a recent job search he was part of for his company, he said, "the person needed to be someone who basically speaks clearly enough for our team to understand him and vice versa. It's basically, we weren't looking for someone who speaks perfect English. We were looking for someone who can communicate. I think that's the important thing. We weren't really looking for how many grammatical mistakes they do or stuff like that."

Communication does not mean you must speak without errors. So don't be afraid or embarrassed if you say something grammatically incorrect during your interview. Trust in your ability and remember that the interviewer can always ask for clarification.

You are speaking too much

This may sound unusual, but in fact, if you are not completely comfortable speaking in English, you probably feel the need to prove your ability in an interview. That insecurity that you feel speaking English manifests itself as a need to give long answers to every question.

Whatever the reason, the result is that you start speaking and keep speaking. Even after you finish answering the question, you keep speaking. Suddenly, you find yourself forgetting what the question was. You lose track of what's important and add unnecessary information to your answer.

This is a good way to lose your interviewer's attention and say something that will be damaging. Think about it: When someone talks for a long time, do you find yourself losing focus? The same is true for your interviewer.

Instead, learn when to stop.

Answer the question and, if appropriate, give an example. But stop talking before you go off-topic. Remember, if the interviewer wants to know more, they can ask you for more information. It is not necessary to say everything before you are prompted. Leave the interviewer space to ask follow-up questions.

Giving just the right amount of information is an important skill to practice before your interview. Practice this by having a clear plan about what you want to express. Think about the examples and stories (more on this later) that you will use and stop speaking when you've completed your plan. Remember the outline we talked about in the previous chapter? Create small outlines in your head before the interview and practice speaking your answers before you go to the interviewer.

You are not answering the right questions

You feel comfortable understanding English, so you might not think too much more when you hear a question from the interviewer. But what they say and what they mean is often slightly different. Only by understanding the meaning can you give the best answer possible.

This problem is not unique to non-native speakers, either. Too many people go into an interviewer without understanding what they are really being asked.

To avoid this mistake, it's crucial to think about the question from the interviewer's perspective. Ask yourself, "What does the interviewer hope to learn about me?" Remember earlier, when we talked about how your interview is not about you? This is where you will apply that principle to show the interviewer you understand that the company is most important.

For example, when the interviewer asks, "Why should we hire you?" They really want to know, "What will you do for our company that the other candidates will not?"

In this example, if you only talk about yourself you are missing an opportunity to stand out. The interviewer needs to know more than just your abilities and qualifications; they need to know you understand the job and goals of their company.

If you don't understand the true meaning of the questions, you are going to answer the wrong questions. This can result in a long, frustrating interview as the interviewer asks for more details. Or a short interview as the interviewer loses interest in you.

Don't forget, the interviewer will have your resume in front of them. They will have read it— because that is their job—before the interview starts. Therefore, you must avoid the temptation to repeat what is on your resume. You are not telling them anything new, and you are not helping them make their decision.

You are not having a conversation

All the hiring professionals I talked to for this book described how difficult it can be to get an interviewee to relax and act naturally. It's easy to feel like your interview is an exam but remember that companies call you for an interview so they can see your personality.

Vanessa from Rise Ventures described this issue in detail:

> "Even in native speakers, interviews in Portuguese, you see that the person is trying to sell themselves all the time. So, I'll say, 'Well, we're looking forward to working with people, not with machines or robots. So let's get to know how you are when you're not too well. What do you do? Do you stay quiet? Do you curse? What can I expect from you when you are in your lowest situation?' And that makes them laugh because I don't think that people ask that at all. So it's like they really want to know what to expect and they loosen up very much in this kind of question. And then they tell us. But we've seen people who don't open up, these people we don't hire."

As we talked about in the last chapter, if you use only the answers you memorized, you will seem insincere or robotic to your interview. You will not engage with the interviewer, and they will notice.

The most important part of your interview is how you connect to the interviewer. You must show them your personality and be able to improvise. Your interviewer also has a responsibility to create a comfortable atmosphere so that you will show your true personality. Both sides want to have an open conversation in an interview.

You may hear a question you hadn't considered or an unexpected joke. Your reactions are important, because at the end of the day, companies are looking for someone who is human.

Companies hire people, not resumes.

Be prepared, but don't worry so much if everything doesn't go how you imagined. Relax, be yourself and don't be afraid to show a little personality.

The importance of telling stories

Imagine you are the interviewer for a moment. You have two final candidates and you think back to their answers. At one point, you asked them both a simple question: "Why should we hire you for this job?" They both gave similar reasons. Here are their answers:

"Well, I think you should hire me because I am very adaptable. This industry is changing every day and every project has different challenges. If you don't adapt to the new challenges, it's impossible to grow as a company. I've worked in this industry for 10 years and I've seen how things have changed. Companies come and go in this industry and you must stay on top of the newest technology and trends if you hope to survive. I know how quickly things can change and I know how to react when things begin to change again. If you hire me, I will bring my expertise and my ability to adapt to this position every day."

The second candidate responded like this:

"You should hire me because of my ability to adapt to new challenges quickly. I've been in this industry for five years and it's changing every day. I remember one time in my old company, we planned an entire project based on using this one software, right? We had a very strict timeline and just as we were beginning to work on the project when … our software crashed. It turned out, even though it was one of the leading programs, the company behind it had gone bankrupt and they stopped updating all their services. So we had to find a new program in a hurry, and no one had used it before! To stay on schedule, I got permission to hire an outside consultant who was an expert with the new program. Our whole team did three days of intensive training on the new software and we got back to work. It was close, but we managed to finish on schedule. I think my ability to adapt and stay calm when there are setbacks makes me unique and well suited for this position."

Both candidates gave good answers. But which candidate do you think you will remember more clearly?

People naturally remember stories

Think back to the people you have met in the past year. Especially those people with whom you've only shared one or two conversations. Which ones do you remember?

You might not even remember the names of some of them, but I bet you remember their stories.

If you can tell good stories during your interview, you will be remembered.[2] The interviewer will not remember the first candidate. Their answer was good and clear, but it was not memorable. The interviewer will remember the second candidate, because they have a story to connect to the person and their answers.

Stories are how we connect to people and connecting to your interviewer is the most important part of any interview. If you can't connect to the person interviewing you, you will not be hired.

Stories also give interviewers something to react to. Look at the two answers above. For the first answer, the interviewer might say, "OK, that's great." But it doesn't leave an opportunity for further discussion.

In contrast, in the second story the interviewer has an opportunity to relate to the story. They might say, "Oh, I remember when that company went bankrupt. It created so many problems for us as well." All of a sudden, you are having a friendly conversation. You are connecting.

Furthermore, stories provide evidence. When you start using stories you are illustrating your experience, not just reciting it.

The interviewer already has your resume; now is your chance to paint a picture and give them an idea of how you act in a professional environment.

There is no doubt the first candidate above is qualified and experienced. In fact, they have five more years' experience than the second candidate. However, if they fail to use stories in their answers, they will have trouble impressing the interviewer. You need to give new information in your interview.

The second candidate may not be as experienced, but they showed the interviewer their ability. They do more than say, "I'm adaptable." They give clear evidence of a time they were forced to adapt. Basically, the interviewer knows more about the second candidate and can imagine their abilities.

The interviewer might ask the first candidate more questions, but they shouldn't have to do the extra work. Make the interviewer's job easier by using stories to provide evidence of your qualities.

In her best-selling book, "Stories that Stick: How Storytelling Can Captivate Customers, Influence Audiences, and Transform Your Business," storytelling expert Kindra Hall talks about how crucial stories are in many contexts. She shares many examples from her own experience about how stories can "bridge the gap" between the storyteller and their audience. In this case, you and your interviewer.

She writes, "Never underestimate the power your story has over the competition. When the stakes are highest, come prepared to tell stories and watch the results follow."[3]

Hall gives countless examples of how stories have helped bridge the gap between fundraisers and donors, businesses and clients, and yes, even interviewees and interviewers. Stories are essential to the way we communicate, and you must not go into your interview without having a few different stories ready.

Preparing good stories should be a part of your preparation and practice for an interview. It is difficult to think of stories at the moment you are asked a question. And you will have the opportunity to tell stories in your interview (more on this later). So don't forget to start thinking of specific situations that illustrate your better qualities.

We will learn more about the exact stories you should have ready later in the book. But be prepared to talk about your failures at your past jobs, your problem-solving skills and how you act as a leader.

The STAR Method

If you're worried about how to form a strong story in English for your interview, think about the STAR Method. The STAR method is an interview technique designed to help you tell effective and well-organized stories in your interview.

S - Situation
T - Task
A - Action
R - Result

In the first part of your answer, you explain the situation. Tell the interviewer what was happening at the time of the story you're about to tell. Was your company in the middle of a crisis? Was there a new product being launched? Give context to your story so that the rest of the story is clear.

Next, you will explain the task. What did you need to do in this situation? This will help the interviewer understand your goal in this story.

Explain the action you took in this situation. This part of your story will be slightly longer than the two before. Use details to show your interviewer exactly what you did. Explain how you solved the issue or found a solution. Remember to be precise.

Finally, explain the results of your action. Use specific numbers when possible. Tell the interviewer what the outcome of your actions were. What did you achieve in this situation?

This is a great way to keep your stories organized and concise. The whole answer does not have to take a long time. Most stories will be between 2-3 minutes. Using this format and practicing before your interview will prepare you to tell informative stories.

Doing your research

Everyone will tell you that you need to research the company before an interview. And of course, this is absolutely true. But it's also true that a simple web search and a quick look at the company website is not nearly enough.

Before we talk about the things you need to know about the company, let's talk about why you need to research the company. There are several reasons, but they all come back to two primary motives

You need to show the company you are interested in what it does, and you need to show its employees you understand the company culture.

In today's competitive job market, companies do not need to hire anyone that walks in the door with the right skills. If a person does not even take the time to learn about the company, the company has no reason to hire them.

Think of it this way: If you go on a first date with someone and they do not make an effort to learn about your interests, are you going to go on a second date with them? The only difference with a job interview is that you need to research before the first interview.

Understanding company culture is the second main reason it's important to do your research well. Company culture includes values and expectations and determines what kind of workplace environment the job will provide.[4] It's also becoming increasingly important to modern companies.

If you don't understand the company culture, it will be difficult to show your interviewer that you will be a good choice for the vacancy.

It's also important to think about yourself when you are researching the company. Before thinking about how you will use your research in the interview, you need to ask yourself whether you will be happy working in that company for an extended period.

You deserve to be happy with the job you are doing, and companies deserve to have happy, productive workers. Thorough research can protect both you and the employer from an unsuccessful partnership.

For now, let us assume you know enough about the company to want to work there. What specific information should you know before your interview?

Most importantly, you need to have a good understanding of the company culture and values. This means knowing what a normal day in the office will be like. You should know whether there is a strict corporate structure in which you are expected to bring ideas only to your direct boss, or a more horizontal structure where any employee is encouraged to share ideas directly with the company leadership.

This research will help you understand what the company expects from its employees.

You also must have a clear idea of what your responsibilities will be if you are offered the role. This information will mostly come from the job description, but you have a responsibility to make sure you understand the position. Understanding the company culture will help you understand what your potential job entails.

You must demonstrate that you did your research during the interview. Knowing enough about the company before the interview will allow you to show that you are sincerely interested in the position and will allow you to ask meaningful questions. In the next section of this book, we will talk about how to use this information to show you are a strong candidate.

A checklist of what you should know before the interview

Essential information:

- Basic company information (locations, number of employees, main products, etc.)
- The company's main values
- The skills required for the position
- Responsibilities of the position
- The company's main competitors and challenges

Extra information:

- Information about office culture (from current or former employees)
- The company's goals and ambitions
- Company policies and procedures

About your interviewer

The first time I was in a position where I needed to interview candidates, I was terrified. I was young and inexperienced, and I did not feel qualified to decide who got a job. I barely felt qualified to do the job myself. I didn't know what questions to ask or even what I was looking for. I was more nervous than my interviewees.

I interviewed six candidates on the first day. Every one of them had the skills for the job; we made sure of that before inviting them to interview. But only one that day felt like the person who would make a good addition to our team. I knew it about halfway through the interview when the conversation started to flow easily.

Throughout your career, you will be interviewed by professional hiring managers, team leaders and CEOs. Sometimes, they will be great at interviewing; other times, they will be just as nervous as you are. You may encounter other non-native English speakers, this a multi-national company after all. You may even interview with someone with fewer language skills than you have. But every time you go to an interview, you will be speaking with another human being.

Interviewers are not machines (yet). They are the same kind of person you already work with every day in your current job or school. They have different personalities and their own strengths and flaws. It's easy to see the interviewer as someone above you, but don't forget that on another day, your positions could be reversed.

This is important to remember. You want to connect with the human across from you in an interview. After you get past the first round, you will likely interview with your future team leaders and members. They are looking for the person they will enjoy working with.

You must recognize the interviewer's humanity in unpleasant

situations as well. Maybe the interview doesn't go well, but that doesn't mean it was your fault. Interviewers also sleep poorly sometimes or feel slightly ill on the day of the interview.

So, what should you expect from your interviewer?

First, be ready for anything. There is no way to know what kind of interviewer you will have or what kind of day they are having. However, there are some common traits a good interviewer will display.

You should expect that they have already read your resume. They probably have a copy in front of them if they need to remind themselves of something. You do not need to repeat everything when you introduce yourself.

A good interviewer will try to help you feel comfortable and relaxed. They want to see how you act naturally. Interviewers are looking for the person you will be in the office, not the refined version of yourself you are in an interview.

To do this, an interviewer may begin with small talk or ask you a lighthearted question at some point during the interview. They will try to ask questions you can't possibly have prepared for to see how you react in the moment.

Interviewers will give you chances to ask questions. This usually happens near the end, but a good interviewer will give you opportunities throughout the interview. Don't be afraid to use them to ask intelligent questions. Remember, you want to have a conversation.

It also helps to think of the interview from the interviewer's perspective. Their job is to hire the best person for the company —someone who will fit in with the office culture and do the required work productively. When you prepare for your interview, consider how your answers sound with this in mind. Avoid unnecessary information, and always think about the company's needs first.

"I think that [the interviewer] needs to try to make it comfortable for everyone, as informal as you can so people can relax and be themselves. It is a stressful situation for the applicant to be evaluated like that." Says Petteri Nakamura.

You don't need to be intimidated by your interviewer. They are a human being there to get to know you.

Part II: The Interview

Introducing yourself

Tell me about yourself.
Can you please introduce yourself?
Can you tell us a little about yourself?

You've arrived at the interview on time and appropriately dressed. You're 15 minutes early, of course, and you finally get called into the room. Congratulations, this is it! Everything you've been preparing for is happening now.

And you know as soon as you walk into the interview, it is time to talk about yourself and how you can serve the company.

Almost every interview will begin with an introduction. They may say "tell me about yourself" or "can you please introduce yourself," but no matter the phrasing the question is the same. This will be your prompt to begin the answer you've prepared.

How you introduce yourself will determine the tone of the rest of the interview. First impressions are made quickly, and they are difficult to change. In fact, some human resources professionals report making their decision about a candidate within the first five minutes of a job interview.[5] A strong introduction can go a long way toward helping you secure a job.

So, do not bore your interviewer in your introduction. Because you've reached the interview stage, it's safe to assume your interviewer has read your resume and reviewed your social media presence. They know why you're in the room, and that's good, because you've already gotten further than most candidates.

Now is the time to show your personality and ability to work in this company. Do not repeat what they already know about you. Tell them a story about yourself to show why you're the person for the job.

Your introduction must include a few key elements.

First, you will give a brief background about your expertise and qualifications. Remember, do not repeat your resume. Do not go back to the beginning of your employment history and talk about your first job. It is a lot easier than that. Repeat your name and say how long you have worked in your field. That's it.

For example, I might say, "My name is James, and I am a professional interview coach with four years of experience." Or, "I'm James, and I've been working as a professional interview coach for the past four years."

Then, move into the middle part of your answer. This is the part where you will highlight the traits and experiences that make you suitable for the job. You will also introduce the talking points that you will reinforce throughout your interview.

This part of your answer is a little more flexible. You can choose to highlight your best qualities or your most relevant experience. I recommend focusing on your best character traits. Show the interviewer how you think of yourself and what you will offer the company if you are hired. Whatever you say, try to support your answer with short stories or examples.

For example, I usually say, "I think of myself as an excellent communicator. When I worked at a public school in Thailand after university, none of my co-workers spoke English very clearly. That's when I learned that language skills and communication skills are two different abilities. I had to learn how to communicate with my colleagues, and this is a skill I've continued to develop."

At the end of your answer, it's a good idea to say which job you are applying for and to give a short reason. You will have more opportunities to talk about why you want to work here, so keep it brief. Alternatively, you can offer a reason you are a good fit for this company. Here's an example.

"I believe my extensive experience and excellent communication skills make me well suited to work as a community relations manager here at TOP Athletics."

Most importantly, everything you say should be connected to the position you are applying for. Choose your best qualities that are useful for your desired position.

One of the most common questions I get from clients is about how long their introduction should be. The time will vary, but you should expect to speak between one to two minutes. Any longer than that and you risk losing your interviewer's attention. Here's a full example:

> "So, my name is James and I've worked in digital marketing for seven years now. I specialize in running effective Google ad campaigns and consistently create a 15% or higher return on investment. I think of myself as a team player. I believe the only way to produce consistent results is to work with other departments. In my current job, I make a point to meet every week with the sales department, so I can always understand their goals and use that knowledge to shape our current campaigns. Furthermore, I always try to stay up to date on the latest trends. I take part in several communities where we discuss the changes and advances in the industry. I think it's crucial to be up to date to maintain a competitive edge in this fast-paced market. I truly believe my ability to work in a team and my constant desire to learn will make me a valuable asset to your company."

Useful phrases:

- "I think of myself as…"
- "I like to think I'm…"
- "If you hire me, I will…"
- "I am a [title] with [#] years of experience."
- "I'd be a great addition to your team because…"
- "…a valuable asset to your company."
- "…a great/strong addition to your team."

- "... I hope to bring my skills and experience to your company."

Talking about your experience

Tell me about your work experience.
Can you talk about your past experience?
What can you tell us about your experience?
Why should we choose you for this position?

Often, the only difference between you and the other candidates for the position is your work experience. Everyone might have the same qualifications and certifications, but what you did at your previous jobs is unique. Everyone has the degree that you have, but no one else achieved what you did in your last job.

This is one of the ways you will show the interviewer you are the best candidate.

Interviewers will always be looking for what makes you unique and different from other applicants. Don't be afraid to talk about the specifics of your past work. Tell them about your responsibilities, office environment and, most importantly, talk about what you have accomplished. Talk about the results of your hard work and how you helped the company's mission.

Remember, the more specific the better. Use numbers and tangibles to show your value.

For example, if you want to show how your marketing campaign increased revenue for the company, don't leave out the details. Tell the interviewer the exact percentage increase between the quarter before your campaign and the quarter after.

Also, remember to choose the most relevant work experience. Don't talk about your customer service experience if you're applying for a programming job. Talk about the work you have done related to the position you want.

You may or not be asked to speak about your experience directly. But even if the interviewer doesn't ask you to talk about your experience, you will still talk about your past work in other parts of the interview.

Your work experience is what you will discuss throughout the interview, not just at the beginning. You can talk about your experience when asked about your strengths and weaknesses or when you're answering "tell me about a time …" questions later in the interview. Remember, your experience is an asset, and you want to share it every opportunity you have. Let's look at one example:

> "Well, I'm a project manager with 10 years' experience. I've had a lot of successes and failures in this time, of course, but I always do what's best for my company. In my most recent job, I supervised the release of a new pharmaceutical drug for the whole Western European market. It was the biggest project I've managed in my career and I'm happy to say it went well. The project ended on schedule, and the initial sales surpassed our estimates by almost 25% in the first quarter. Before working in pharmaceuticals, I managed projects in the tech industry and the automotive industry. The teams I've managed have been less than 10 people and sometimes larger than 200. I've worked with all different kinds of people, and I'm good at finding a way to communicate with them. Throughout my career, I've learned to communicate across teams and manage expectations. I think my management abilities are my greatest asset and I look forward to using my experience and skills to help projects run smoothly at your company."

But what if you don't have any experience?

Maybe you're a recent graduate and you haven't worked in a company before. Or perhaps you're trying to switch to a different area and you're thinking, "How can I talk about my experience if I don't have any?"

Let's talk about being a recent graduate first. Sometimes it feels like companies ask recent college graduates for five years of experience. It feels like everything is against you.

Fortunately, a lot of businesses out there really do want to hire young, talented applicants and help them develop into important members of the team. Look for these companies for your first job. Remember, no one has much experience when they apply for their very first position.

When you get to the interview and they ask you to talk about your experience, focus on your relevant classwork. If you've had an internship, talk extensively about what you learned and what your responsibilities were. Focus on the new skills you acquired and how you adapted to a professional working environment.

Beyond that, if you are interviewing for your first job, talk about your enthusiasm for learning new skills and your own professional development. Talk about how you envision your career path and how you want to help the company immediately and in the future.

You are an investment for the company, and if they think you're a good investment, they will be eager to hire you. Let's read an example:

> "Well, I just graduated in May with a degree in finance and accounting from the University of Madrid, so I haven't had the chance to work full-time yet. However, in my final semester, I was fortunate to be an intern in a small accounting firm here in Madrid. We mostly served small businesses and some individuals, but I was able to learn firsthand how to manage an audit from start to finish. I took advantage of every opportunity I had to go to meet our clients and watch my supervisor working. By the end of the internship, my boss allowed me to compile reports on my own. So, I think this experience, combined with my studies, will make me a great employee here at Deloitte. I'm eager to learn and I pick things up quickly. I am a hard worker and I know I can do well in a supportive environment like the one Deloitte is

known for."

And what about if you are changing fields? How can you talk about your experience if you are applying for a job in a completely different area?

This is actually becoming more common, which means recruiters and interviewers are more open to the idea. Several of my clients have switched career paths or industries successfully, and how you talk about your experience in the interview is crucial in this process.

You will need to relate your actual experience with the skills that will be needed in your new job. Even if the industry is completely different, many of the skills will likely be the same. Your job is to communicate your ability to complete the required tasks using the skills you already possess. In addition, you will stress your ability to learn using examples of skills you have learned in the past.

Another strategy you'll want to use is to focus on your soft skills. Your soft skills are the characteristics that allow you to interact with other people. They differ from hard skills which are easily quantifiable and can be taught in a formalized manner. Examples of soft skills include adaptability, teamwork, motivation and communication skills.

Almost every industry and every job require people with good communication skills. All businesses are looking for leaders who will move up in the company. These are just two examples that apply to most jobs; there are many more.

Lacking experience is not always a negative. Many companies understand the value of having someone who enters a job with a new perspective and a willingness and ability to learn. Even for a higher level position, hiring someone from the outside offers a fresh perspective for companies that have been struggling to adapt to changing markets. This is the reason companies search for CEOs from different companies rather than promote someone internally. Do not let your lack of experience or experience in an industry deter you from applying for your dream job.

One last thing. Clients often ask me, what is the difference between the questions "tell me about yourself" and "tell me about your experience?"

I get this question a lot, and, sometimes, they will not ask you both of these questions. Especially if you address your experience in your introduction. However, you still need to be ready to talk about your experience throughout the interview. The main difference is that in your introduction, you should focus on your personality. When talking about experience, focus on your achievements and specific projects.

Showing that you did your research

What do you know about our company?
Why do you want to work here?
What makes you the best person for this position?

The quickest way for an interviewer to find out you are not interested in a job is to discover you did not do your research. It will be obvious to them sooner or later and it will make the rest of the interview uncomfortable. It's a sign of disrespect, and there is no excuse to go into an interview without at least basic knowledge of the company and position.

A friend of mine who works at an international nonprofit recently did four phone interviews. I was fortunate enough to be able to listen in. One interview was notably shorter than the others. When she got off the call I asked what went wrong. "He had to ask, 'which position is this interview for again?'" she told me. You may think these things only happen in YouTube videos about bad interviews. But here I was hearing it firsthand. Don't be the person who doesn't know about the job in the interview.

By the way, the other three candidates were sent to the next round of the process. The candidate who didn't do their research was the only one eliminated at that stage.

Good research and use of what you have learned can just as easily give you an advantage over other candidates. You will use your knowledge of the company and the position to show you are the candidate best suited for the job.

Your first opportunity to show your knowledge is when the interviewer asks you, "What do you know about our company?"

It's not enough to recite the facts you memorized from the company website. The interviewer doesn't care that you know when the company was founded or how many employees they have. This isn't the information that matters.

Instead, show what you know about the company's goals and work culture. Show them that you know about their current initiatives and projects. This will show your interviewer that you did your research well and are interested in what the company is doing.

Next, you must go one step further and talk about why you think the company goals or values are important. Connect your research to your own values and goals. By expressing a connection between your values and the company's values, you will leave a strong impression on your interviewer.

What does this look like? Let's look at two examples below where the candidates show their knowledge of a company's goals.

Candidate one says:

> "Well, I know that this bank strives to be the most accessible in Spain and to provide intuitive solutions to clients in every part of the country. I know that your company supports initiatives in rural areas and focuses on customer experience. I also know that [company name] is on the leading edge of mobile banking technology and that you want to expand this area in the next five years. I think mobile banking is the future and I appreciate how [company] invests so heavily in this area in order to facilitate transactions and simplify sending and receiving money anywhere in the world."

Candidate two says:

> "Well, as we both know, the future of banking will be based on mobile technologies and I know [company name] is the leader in this area. This is what inspired me to apply for your company. When I was growing up, I lived in a small town and there were only one or two ATMs in the whole area. In order to send money, we had to drive to a neighboring town. When I went to university and started working, it was

almost impossible to send money back to my parents. When this company introduced their mobile app in 2014, it made it so much easier for my parents and the other people in my town. I've seen firsthand the importance of accessible banking, and that's why there is no company I would rather work for than [company name]."

Again, the first answer is not *bad*. But the second candidate not only tells a story, but explains why the goals of the company are important to them personally. Both candidates show they know important facts about the company, but only one makes a personal connection with the company goals. The first answer is more a regurgitation of facts you may find on a press release. The second answer shows knowledge with use of dates and understanding of the overall strategies of the bank.

This also applies when talking about company values. Every young company these days will make a point to share their values on their website. You can find this mostly on the "Careers" page for larger corporations and the "Our Story" or "About Us" page for smaller businesses. It's not a secret, and therefore it's not impressive to share that you know about their values. To impress the interviewer, you once again must connect your values to those of the company. For example:

"I know that your company was founded in 2017 to address the gap in the market in last-mile transportation. Your proprietary electric scooters can be activated by any paying client with your mobile app and are great for accessing almost any area in the city. I know you have plans to expand to five more major cities before the end of the year as well. More importantly, I know that inside the company you value your horizontal structure and the free communication of ideas. This is something that really attracted me to your company, because in my previous job it was very difficult to share ideas with the executives. To get anything done, you had to talk to your manager, and they would talk to their manager and ... well, you get the idea. Change wouldn't happen for weeks and it felt like we were moving slowly. Having a more horizontal structure will allow me to work together with my team to see the results of our work quickly. I think this is one of the best things about your company and I hope I can be part of this office culture."

Of course, this question is not your only chance to prove that you did your research. You must always be looking for opportunities to demonstrate your knowledge.

There's another important question that you will use your knowledge to answer. If you are asked "What makes you the best choice for this position?" or something similar, you need to align yourself with the company goals once again.

This kind of answer is a little different. You will choose one of your best qualities to begin with and connect that to the specific position based on what you've researched.

Remember, you are essentially being asked to compare yourself with other candidates. Choose something that makes you unique. Maybe it's your experience or your ability to solve problems. Try to avoid clichés like you are a "hard worker" (so is everyone else) or that you "work well in a team" (that should be expected for most positions).

Be prepared with your unique selling point and connect it to the position's responsibilities or company values using your research. Here's an example:

"I think I'm the best choice for this position because of my passion for innovation and experience with revolutionary technologies. I know your company is working relentlessly to develop more environmentally friendly aircrafts and I will use my extensive experience to help power this company toward that goal. When I was a designer on the Solar Impulse project, the first electric airplane to circle the globe, everyone told us it was impossible. But my team and I never stopped working hard to develop the technology. I believe your company needs people with my drive and passion to realize its goals. I look forward to applying my skills and work ethic as the lead aeronautical engineer at your company."

The candidate that successfully makes the connection between themselves and the company's values will be the most memorable in an interview. You don't know the other candidates, so you can't really say you are more passionate or more hardworking than they. The best you can do is highlight your best qualities and explain why the company would benefit from your unique traits.

This same idea applies to the question, "Why do you want to work here?" You need to tell a story about your interest in that company. Make the interviewer interested in you as a person and not just your qualifications. Use your knowledge to show genuine interest. If your answer is lacking detail or personality, you will not leave an impression on your interviewer.

If you haven't done your research, just one of these questions will make that fact very obvious to the interviewer. A lack of research can be damaging, but good research can push you to the top of the list. Do the work and use it in your interview.

Useful phrases:

- "I know that your company…"
- "I know this company values…"
- "This company believes in…"
- "…and this is important to me because…"
- "…this value speaks to me because…"
- "…I share this sense of…"
- "…I am passionate about this because…"
- "I look forward to the opportunity to…"
- "I hope to apply all my experience and passion to your team."

- "I will bring this passion to my work in your company."
- "I'm excited to be a part of…"

Thinking forward

Where do you see yourself in five years?
What are your expectations for the future?
What are your long-term career goals?

These days, it seems that staying in one company for your whole career is uncommon, and companies know it. That's why they make extra effort to seek employees that will remain loyal to their company. For you, this is an advantage. Companies are always competing to create a better atmosphere to retain top employees. So when they ask you about your future, you must be honest, but you can express that retaining your services will depend on the opportunities you are offered.

Talking about your experience is usually not enough to get you the job. You must also show that you are capable of thinking about the future.

Almost all interviewers will have a question about the future and, more specifically, your future. The most common of these questions is, "Where do you see yourself in five years?"

Remember, to successfully answer this question, and every question, you must understand why the interviewer wants to know this.

So, think of the company's perspective. Why do companies hire employees at all? And why do they train employees and give them opportunities to grow?

The answer is, they need employees to further the interests of the company. They pay money for professional development and training because they are investing in the people who will improve the company.

Most investments are long-term projects, right? The company doesn't expect you to immediately help them reach new markets and become the top player in the field. But they hope that within five to 10 years you will rise to a higher position and use the new skills you've acquired to help the company grow. In other words, they want to know whether you will be a good investment.

For this reason, they want to hire people who are ambitious and intend to move up in their jobs through the years. This is what you must express when you talk about the future, and remember, you are thinking about the company, not yourself.

Just how important is talking about the future in your interview? Petteri Nakamura, an ICT service manager from Finland, had this to say about a recent interview he was part of:

> "What impressed me about the latest hire was that he—when we asked if he was going to stay in Finland or for how long—he said that staying in Finland is in his five year plan. And I thought, 'woah this guy has a five year plan.' So that was impressive for me. It means that you are actually thinking about where you're going and where you want to go."

Now let's look at an example answer:

> "In five years or so, I hope to earn the title of senior manager. I know that I'm beginning as an associate and it is usually more than five years to achieve that level. But I intend to learn as much as I can in this position, so I can one day help the company from a decision-making position. I believe my commitment to the values of XY Engineering will make me an ideal employee and a great candidate for manager. I am passionate about this work and I want to continue the excellent work XY Engineering has done for the last 38 years."

Include specific details to show the interviewer that you have a plan and you know what it will take to achieve your goals. Remember to focus on what you will do for the company in your future role.

You don't need to lie

Maybe in five years, you see yourself at a different company.

In today's labor market, it's common to change jobs every few years due to a highly competitive and volatile market. Therefore, you may plan to only stay at this company for a couple of years before moving on. If this is you, you do not want to tell your interviewer this.

You always want to be honest during an interview, so how can you express that you are a good investment without lying?

The good news is that companies know the state of the labor market these days and they know that to keep top talent (you) they need to make the position and benefits attractive. You will use this to your advantage.

So, tell the truth, but leave the possibility open that your future will be in this company. Talk about your desire to improve yourself and desire to help the company grow in the future. You don't have to be thinking exactly five years in the future.

Leave the past in the past

If you are currently working in a company, it's natural that your interviewer will ask you why you want to leave that company. For this question, it is a good idea to focus on the future instead of the past.

For starters, do not say anything negative about your current company. I need to repeat that: Do not say anything bad about your current company. Maybe you've had a terrible experience there and your boss is terrible, but for these questions it's crucial to leave the past in the past and focus on the future.

As soon as you say something bad about your current company, the interviewer will be thinking about the things you will say about their company in your next interview. Also, especially in specialized areas, you never know what might get back to your current boss.

Here's a simple rule to follow: Don't say anything you would not say to your current boss's face.

Focus on the future by talking about new challenges and opportunities you would have at the new company that you didn't have at the old company. It makes sense to move to a company that provides more opportunities for development and learning, and your current bosses will understand that as well.

Be honest, but focus on the positives and thinking forward rather back. Let's look at an example.

> "I don't necessarily want to leave my current job. I'm very grateful for the opportunities I've had there, and the work environment is great. However, when your recruiter called me I thought a lot about why this would be a good move for me. In my current company, I am comfortable with my work and I rarely face new situations anymore. In this position, I look forward to the opportunity to work with new technologies and bigger clients. I've managed big accounts in my current job, but the accounts at your company will provide a new challenge and allow me to push myself in my professional development. I'm ready for the next step in my career, and I believe working here will be good for me and that I can help this company continue its tradition of excellence and quality."

Useful phrases:

- "In the future I want to…"
- "In five years, I hope to be…"
- "I would like to be…"
- "If I'm given the opportunity…"
- "I want to grow so I can help this company…"
- "I want to develop my skills as a…"
- "I want to use the skills I develop here to…"
- "…so I can help this company expand their…"

- "...in order to help this company achieve..."
- "...to maintain the competitive position of this company."

Talking about your strengths and weaknesses

What do you consider your greatest strength?
What do you think is your biggest weakness?
Tell me about an area in which you would like to improve.
What is one skill you would like to improve?

Every interviewer will ask you about your strengths and your weaknesses. Both of these questions serve a unique purpose that helps the interviewer understand your character. Let's talk about each of them.

First, you will mention your strengths before they specifically ask you about them. In fact, you will start to reference your strengths in the very first answer. Remember when we talked about your main "talking points"? Your biggest strength is one of these and, as a result, a common theme throughout your interview.

What is the interviewer looking for with this question?

Most importantly, they want to know that you have the skills for this job. Therefore, you must choose a strength that is relevant to the position. Do not talk about your programming ability if you are applying to a manager position. Choose your leadership ability or communication skills instead.

The strength you choose needs to be important for the job.

Your answer will also tell the interviewer how much you understand the position. By choosing a necessary skill, you are showing that you did your research and know what qualities are necessary for the role.

When you answer this question, it is important to remember to illustrate your strength. Do not just say you are a strong leader and stop speaking. Give an example of a time you used your leadership skills to get a positive result.

Example: "My greatest strength is my skilled leadership. In my last job, I improved employee retention in my department by 80% during my time there. I think I achieved this by being a good listener and taking time to understand the concerns and goals of each one of my team members. I enjoy being the one to lead and make tough decisions and I know I will do that well at your company."

There are countless ways to answer this question. This example works because the interviewee shows a real outcome of their leadership skills. They give a reason they believe they are a strong leader, and at the end they refer back to the job they are applying for. Think about these elements when you are preparing your own answer.

One more thing clients often as me is, "How many strengths should I mention?"

Usually you will just need to talk about one, but pay attention to how the interviewer asks the question. If they say "tell me about your biggest strength" it's best to choose just one and give a little more detail. If they use the plural "strengths" you may choose two or a maximum of three. However, you still have the choice to focus on your most important skill. No matter what you choose, remember to give some details for each strength.

Useful phrases:

- "My greatest strength is ..."
- "I accomplished/achieved this by ..."
- "I hope to have the opportunity to apply my [strength] skills in your company."

Now let's talk about questions about your weaknesses. It's easy to be confused by this question. You may wonder why this question is so common. Nobody wants to admit their weakness, right? Surely people lie when asked this question.

In fact, this question is starting to become less common. Instead, interviewers are choosing to ask a similar question such as, "Where is one area in which you would like to improve?" The point of the question doesn't change, so let's talk about how to approach this answer.

How you answer this question will tell your interviewer a lot about you. If the candidate lies, the interviewer will still learn something. You should not lie, because the interviewer has heard it before and will know you are not being honest.

It is best to be authentic and honest for every question in your interview, and this one is no exception. Of course, you must still choose something that will not be a warning sign to the interviewer.

Just like you chose something relevant for the question about your strengths, you must not choose a crucial skill for your weakness. If you are applying for a job as an accountant, do not say you have poor organization skills. Instead, choose a weakness that is honest but not something absolutely required for the job.

Also, do not try the common trick of choosing a "weakness" that is actually a positive. Too many people say their weakness is that they are a "perfectionist" or, even worse, that they "care too much." This overused strategy is outdated and will tell your interviewer that you are not introspective and are scared to admit your real weakness. They will also learn that you researched how to answer this question. Do not do this.

So what should you choose?

As long as you are honest and it's not an absolutely crucial skill, it doesn't really matter what you choose to say as your weakness.

What really matters in this answer is how you are improving on that weakness. Whatever you choose, you need to give clear steps and examples of what you are doing to improve yourself.

For example, if you say that your weakness is public speaking, you need to talk about the seminar you attended to work on this skill and the ones you plan to do in the future. Be specific and use this question as an opportunity to show your desire to improve.

Example: "I'm not the most organized person, and I know sometimes it can affect my productivity. I sometimes struggle to keep my desk clean or my schedule organized. However, this year I started scheduling time on Mondays to organize my week, and it's been very helpful. It's a new habit for me so I'm still working on it, but I've already noticed I have more time to prepare for calls and I don't feel as stressed by last-minute surprises I forgot about. It's something I hope to keep working on this year."

This example works because the interviewee doesn't try to hide behind a weakness that is actually a strength. Still, the key is recognizing why it's a weakness and talking about strategies for improving. This would not be a good answer if you were applying for a job as an office manager or another role that requires precise organizational skills. But for many positions, this would work. Remember, talking about your improvement is the most important part of your answer. Also, this answer will be short and to the point. There is no reason to speak at length about your weaknesses.

Useful phrases:

- "I sometimes have trouble…"
- "I often struggle to…"
- "I'm working on this by…"
- "I'm making an extra effort to…"
- "It's something I continue to work on every day."

Should I talk about my English as a weakness?

Almost every client I have worked with has asked me if they should mention their English as a weakness. My answer is always the same. I say, be more specific.

If you say your English ability is your weakness, it presents two major problems for your interviewer. First, English is the language of operation in this position. You will use it every day and are expected to be proficient. Admitting that you consider yourself a weak English user will only make your interviewer concerned about your ability to do the job. Second, saying you struggle to communicate in English while communicating in proficient English can be confusing. It will certainly feel insincere. It will feel like you chose this answer to avoid giving a more accurate answer and admitting a greater weakness. In other words, saying that your weakness is your English ability will not have the desired effect.

However, if you choose a more specific skill, you will have the opportunity to express your hard work without giving concern to the interviewer. Instead of saying, "my English is weak," try choosing a specific skill to talk about. For example, you can say, "Sometimes I feel nervous when I need to present in English." Or "Speaking on the phone in English can be a challenge." (Of course, don't say this if the job will require a lot of phone calls!)

Example: "Sometimes I feel insecure when I need to present to a large group in English. Although I feel confident in one-on-one situations and group meetings, speaking to a group can be intimidating. To overcome this, I put extra effort into preparing and planning my presentations when I know they will be in English. Often, I will prepare too much even for the smallest presentations. Rehearsing my presentations helps me master this fear."

Most importantly, follow the advice above and focus on the concrete steps you are taking to improve these skills. You can even say you are working with an English coach online. Be specific and be honest and you will leave a good impression with this answer.

Tell me about a time ... questions

Remember earlier when we talked about why it's important to tell stories? This is a useful skill for many different questions, but for this next type, it is an absolute necessity. These are known as behavioral interview questions.

These questions begin with "tell me about a time ..." and they come in many forms. Some of the most common examples are:

Tell me about a time you faced a challenge at work.
Tell me about a time you worked in a team.
Tell me about a time you had to exercise your leadership skills.
Tell me about a time you failed.
Tell me about a time you made a mistake.
Tell me about a time you dealt with a difficult client.

Using a general answer does not work for this type of question. You cannot talk about what you do any time that you encounter this situation. The only satisfactory answer comes in the form of a story. You need to talk about one specific time.

When I first introduce this type of question to my client, I get a lot of generalities. They begin their answer saying, "Well, when I have a difficult client I always try to ..." or, "Whenever I make a mistake the first thing I do is ..."

If you start like this, you've already missed the point of the question. Do not make this mistake. Think of a specific instance for these situations before your interview and be ready to adapt your story to the question you are asked.

I know this kind of answer is challenging for non-native speakers. In fact, it's challenging for everyone. Typically, these kinds of answers will be the longest, and therefore it is easy to get confused if you make a mistake. To avoid getting off-topic or panicking in the middle of your answer, you need to have a clear plan.

Earlier, we talked about the STAR method to help create strong stories. In this chapter we will look at the most basic elements.

First of all, you need to have a plan. A good story has a clear beginning, middle and end. By practicing a clear structure, your stories will have more impact and illustrate your strengths well.

The beginning of your story should provide context. Tell the interviewer when the story takes place, what project you were working on and any other important details to make the story clear. As always, be specific. Instead of "sometime last year," you can say, "last June." Instead of describing the project as "a campaign to increase page views," you want to say, "a campaign to increase page views by targeting 20-30 year old professionals in Sao Paulo and Rio de Janeiro using targeted Facebook and Instagram ads." You don't need to give all the details, but you need to give enough to make sure the rest of the story makes sense.

The middle of the story should talk about the action you took. What did you do to resolve the problem? What specific actions did you take, and why did you do them? The goal of these questions is to understand how you think. The interviewer wants to know about your reasoning ability and whether it is compatible with the company.

Again, be specific and focus on your part in the story. This question is about you. Your interviewer does not need to know what your team members or supervisors did. They want to know about your thinking process.

The middle part, where you talk about your actions, should be the longest part of your story. If it is not, consider giving less context and getting into the middle sooner. Because this is the most important part of the story, you want to spend more time going into detail to show how you handled the situation.

At the end of your story, you need to share the results of your actions. Ask yourself this: What did you achieve through your actions?

Sharing the result is a crucial part of the story. You would not tell a joke without a punchline. There must be a point to your story you share at the end. Something to show that what you did produced a positive outcome.

Use numbers and figures when you can. Do not just say "we successfully increased the number of page views." Tell the interviewer exactly how big the increase was compared to the previous period. For example, you can say, "After the campaign, there was a 30% increase in page views and a 7% increase in conversions." The more detailed you can be, the better.

The stories you choose should be true, of course, and they should highlight your best qualities. You have the power to choose which stories to tell. Most importantly, make sure you start to think of stories before you arrive at the interview. These questions should not be a surprise to you, and, just like the other questions, you should be ready. Preparing the right stories is an important part of your interview practice.

Now let's look at an example.

> "One time I faced a big challenge at work was last summer when my boss told me our team was being downsized. I was asked to review everyone on my team and decide which employees should be cut and which should stay. Because we were so close as a team, this was incredibly difficult for me to do. I started to call each employee into my office for a private meeting to talk about their performance. I didn't tell them that we were forced to downsize because I didn't want the office to start gossiping. Otherwise, I did everything I could to make each member feel valued. After telling my decisions to my boss, he asked that I be the one to let them go. I met separately with each employee and explained as clearly as possible the reasons we needed to downsize and why they were chosen to leave. I also made it clear that it was not a problem with their work, but with factors beyond our con-

trol. I promised to send them my sincerest recommendation and be there for any questions they had. It was a difficult challenge, but as a result of my clear communication the employees we let go were understanding and respected that I told them myself. My boss was happy to see I was capable of making difficult decisions, and I believe my team started to appreciate me more for my honesty and the way I handled the situation. This was important, because it allowed us to continue our work without too much interruption."

This example does a good job at showing a real, honest challenge that many people in leadership roles can relate to. Notice how the candidate focuses a lot on their actions and explains in detail what they did in this situation. The story has three clear parts and includes all the most important information without going beyond what is necessary.

When telling stories, it is also important to be careful that you do not speak for too long. It is especially easy with this kind of question to go off-topic or forget your organization.

To avoid this, you want to prepare your plan before the interview and practice telling these stories as much as possible. It also helps to refer back to the question throughout your answer. In the example above, notice how the candidate refers to "the challenge" in the beginning, middle and end of his story. The theme of the story is clear throughout the answer, and the storyteller stays strictly on topic. There are no unnecessary details; we don't even learn why the team was being downsized. The story is concise and would probably take about two minutes to tell.

Likewise, you do not have to speak for a long time, even though this will be slightly longer than your typical answer. Instead of worrying about how long you will speak, worry about including all the important details in your story. If you include all the crucial information about the context, your actions and the result, the story will sound natural and the exact length will not be important.

It's your turn! Asking your interviewer questions

At the end of your interview, you will have an opportunity to ask your interviewer questions. If your interviewer does not give you this opportunity, consider this a big warning sign and think about looking for another company. The interviewer should always ask you something like, "Do you have any questions for us?"

Surprisingly, many people make the mistake of thinking this is an optional question. Candidates do not prepare for this question as they do others. As a result, many interviewees miss an opportunity to finish their interview strongly and leave the best impression.[6]

Like most other questions, this one should not be taken literally. Remember that interviewers want to know that you are interested in working at their company and that you've done your research, and this question is how they learn just how interested you are.

Asking informed questions will show the interviewer that you really want to know more because the job is a serious option for you. It's also one last chance to show them what you already know. Finally, it's a great chance for you to discover any reasons you would *not* want to work there. This opportunity is a benefit for you as much as for the interviewer.

What kind of questions should you ask your interviewer?

One common strategy is to use this chance to find out more details about daily life in the company. You can ask direct questions in this case and find out about your interviewer's perception of the company. This is especially a good idea if you have passed the first round of interviews with human resources and you are interviewing with someone who works in the same department as your potential position.

This kind of question shows you are thinking about how you would do the job and that the idea of working in their company is exciting. Don't be afraid of asking for too much information. The interviewer may politely decline to share something, but you will be surprised how much information you can discover with the right questions. Here are some example questions:

Can you tell me what a typical day for someone on this team is like?
How would you describe the atmosphere in the office?
What is your favorite part about working in this company?
Which other departments or team members will I work most closely with?

It's also a good idea to ask about the future and your potential career path. It makes sense that you want to know your prospects if you are accepted for this role. After all, you are probably not applying for the role you want to stay in forever.

This kind of question can help show your ambition. Also, you are expressing that you can see yourself in this company for an extended time if you have good professional development opportunities. The interviewer will be happy to provide you with the possibilities of your position because they know talent is difficult to keep in today's labor market. Take a look at some possible questions:

Does this company offer professional development opportunities? What can I expect in this regard?
What are some companies or positions that previous employees here have moved onto?
What are the company's plans for this department in the future?

Another theme you can ask about relates to company culture and expectations in the office. With this topic, be careful not to ask questions you should already know the answer to. However, you may ask for more details regarding important values, especially to see the perspective of your interviewers. Here are some examples:

How do you measure success in this company? What about in this position specifically?
What do you believe is the most important value in this company?
What qualities do the most successful people in this company share? What do you look for?
What do you think is the most challenging thing about working in this company?

It's definitely worth asking whether the interviewer has any concerns about you or your qualifications as well. It might seem direct, but don't be afraid to ask something like, "Are there any concerns you have about me as a candidate?"

This question shows that you are invested in the position and will give you a chance to respond and prove your value. It also shows that you are introspective and are comfortable thinking about self-improvement. Exact questions include:

Is there anything about my profile that makes you doubt whether I am a good candidate for this role?
Is there anything else I can provide you that would help you make a decision about me?

Finally, it's a good idea to ask about the next steps in the interview process, especially if you feel the interview went well. This will show your enthusiasm and eagerness to continue speaking with this company. Many interviewers will offer this information at the end, so make sure you give them the opportunity to do so before asking.

As a bonus, the answer to this question will help you write your follow-up email, which we will discuss in the next section. Consider ending your conversation with one of the questions below:

Can you tell me when I can expect to hear from you?
If I pass this stage, what can I do to prepare for the next steps?

Will I hear from you even if I do not receive an offer?

Questions you should not ask in an interview

In interviews, some questions can damage your chances of getting the job. Some questions will make the interviewer doubt your motivation or commitment. Be careful to avoid questions like these.

What is the salary for this position?

Renata Horvath, a recruiter working in the United Kingdom, says "Believe it or not, sometimes before even I could tell about the position their first question is: What is the salary? I don't like that because I know they are only motivated by money and they would leave the company after two months if they got another offer."

What are the responsibilities of this position?

Avoid asking questions that you should already know the answer to. If you don't already know what your responsibilities would be in this position, you did not do your research well enough.

How soon can I be promoted?

Although there may be a way to ask this that comes across as ambitious, it's better to avoid this question. The interviewer may see you as entitled or unwilling to work in the position they are offering.

How often do you have performance reviews?

This is a question that will be answered when you start at the company. Asking this in your interview may make your interviewer concerned. They will wonder if you are insecure about receiving feedback.

Any questions about vacation time or benefits.

Your interview is a time to impress your interviewers, not for them to impress you with the offer just yet. You may already have an idea of the benefits from the job offer from websites like Glassdoor that offer insights into different companies. As for vacation time, asking about this will raise questions about your commitment to the work. Save this discussion for your orientation with human resources after there is an offer on the table.

Answering a question when you don't know the answer

Recently, I was in consultation with a client and they asked me a question that I didn't know the answer to. It happens occasionally, because no one knows everything. And because I work with clients from different fields, I'm often faced with new terms and unfamiliar processes.

So how did I answer? I promise I didn't lie and try to sell it as the truth. If I did that, I wouldn't have many clients.

Instead, I admitted I didn't know the answer. I told the truth. And then I explained what I thought about the question and mentioned I would research it more thoroughly before our next session. Of course, I followed through with this promise. As a result, I learned something new, and the client got an honest and up-to-date answer to her question.

It's impossible to know everything, and there are times in your interview you will be asked a question and you don't have a perfect answer. As technology enters new industries, it's becoming more difficult to know about all the latest tools and news in your industry.

For example, you may know seven different programming languages and be proficient in all of them. But your interviewer might still ask about your experience with an eighth.

When this happens, interviewees tend to respond poorly. They make up a lie about their "proficiency" and try to seem like they know everything. They become flustered and lose their previous confidence.

Obviously, this is a problem for several reasons. First, unless you are an excellent liar, it will be clear you are lying to your interviewer. This is the quickest way to lower your chances of getting a job offer.

Second, if you do manage to fool your interviewer, your lie will soon become apparent if you are hired and expected to work with a skill you do not have. Both outcomes are worse than simply telling the truth.

Fortunately, you don't need to lie if you are asked about a skill you don't have or a question you don't know the answer to. Instead, you can use this situation as an opportunity to highlight your ability to learn.

Let's look at an example.

> "Honestly, I do not know how to use that specific system yet. However, I am confident in my ability to learn quickly and gain proficiency in just a few weeks. In my last position, we took on a project where the client asked us to use Ruby. I had worked with Ruby once or twice before but almost all of my experience involves Python and Java. I had just about three weeks to refresh my skills in Ruby before the coding stage began. But I put in the time both during and outside of work to bring myself up to speed. Because this industry is changing so fast, I always try to stay up to date with the current trends and I trust my ability to learn new skills quickly."

Depending on the industry, eagerness to learn is one of the most sought-after skills in today's job market. Instead of trying to stretch the truth, tell a story. Use an example of something you learned in the past and tell your interviewers how you did it. As always, be specific and use detail. Fortunately, you already have a ready-made example available. You learned an entire second language at some point in your life. Do not underestimate this achievement. Putting yourself in the room to interview for a job in an English-speaking workplace is impressive.

The other strategy you can use is to apply a similar experience to a question. This works if you are asked whether you've ever had an experience in a specific situation. This is another opportunity here you will use a story. Let's look at how this happens:

> "I've never experienced that, so I can't say how I would react, exactly. However, in my last job, we had a similar issue when a client almost pulled out due to an economic downturn. I was the person in charge of the account and they were just about ready to leave. Fortunately, I had a good relationship with the project manager and I explained to him why it was important to continue with the project. I showed him the projections for the finished project, both the best-case and worst-case scenarios in fact. Eventually, I was able to convince him to stay with us. He trusted me because I was always honest with him in the past and was clear about the risks. In the end, the project had a 11% return, which was a bit less than our expectations, but it was still better than if they had pulled out before completion."

This will help you answer questions when you are asked about a skill you haven't learned or a process you're not familiar with. This strategy should help you manage most questions that take you by surprise. Remember, lacking knowledge in some areas is not wrong. In fact, how you answer can turn a perceived negative into a positive.

Part III: After the Interview

Sending follow-up emails

After your interview, it's good practice to send a follow-up email. Most importantly, you need to thank your interviewer. This email should be sent within 24 hours after your interview. It doesn't have to be long. Simply thank the interviewer for their time and for the opportunity.

A follow-up email is also a good opportunity to ask any questions you did not ask during the actual interview. If you need more information about anything, this is your chance to get it.

Your emails should be personal. Find the email of the person who interviewed you and send it to them directly using their name. Do not send a general thank-you email to the hiring team. For example:

Dear Adriana,
I wanted to thank you again for giving me the opportunity to interview with [company name]. I hope I was able to show that I will excel in this position if I am given an offer. Please do not hesitate to ask me if you have any other concerns or need more information from me. Thank you for your time.
Sincerely,
James Jones

Remember, you don't want to send too many emails after the interview. You should always send a thank-you email, and then be patient. It may take a week or longer to receive a response.

Fortunately, most interviewers will tell you when you can expect to hear about the next steps. If they do not respond within the time they initially promised, don't panic! There are hundreds of reasons you may have to wait longer. They could still be interviewing candidates or waiting for a department leader to give their recommendation.

In January, a client of mine interviewed with an international investment bank. Things were moving quickly. What started as a casual conversation with a recruiter soon led to a good conversation with the head of the department. Everything was going well, he told me. The team leader himself was messaging him personally. They talked about the need for urgency and that they wanted to hire him almost immediately. The recruiter said they would be sending an offer before next Friday. It seemed like everything was going perfectly.

Then the next week passed without any communication. I told my client not to worry just yet, there are countless reasons for a small delay. I said let's wait until Monday. Monday came and went, as did Tuesday and my client was starting to worry. I told him it was time to send another email. Of course, he had already sent the thank-you emails we talked about above after each interview. He was diligent and had clearly left a good impression. But now, he was nervous to send another email because he did not want to seem too eager. I pushed him to send a polite email to remind the company of his interest and ask if there was anything else they needed.

The very next day, the company sent a verbal offer and began their background check process. Whatever the reason for the delay, the hiring department just needed a reminder to keep things moving. They likely would have responded to him without his second email, but it may have been another week or even a month! Waiting is uncomfortable and confusing, and you have a right to know one way or the other if you will be offered a job.

If a company does not respond within the time frame they gave you, you should be prepared to send another email. Be polite, and ask again when you can expect an answer. Remember, your time is also valuable, and companies should have respect for your situation as well. Avoid language that sounds accusing or impatient. Here's an example:

Dear Michael,

I just wanted to check in regarding our interview last week. I would be grateful to know if you have decided, or if there is anything else I can provide you with. Thank you again for your time and this opportunity. I look forward to hearing from you.
Sincerely,
Sarah Johnson

Useful phrases for email:

- "I wanted to ..."
    - "reach out to ask about ..."
    - "express my gratitude for ..."
    - "thank you again for the opportunity ..."
    - "check in about ..."
- "Thank you for your time ..."
- "I am writing you ..."
    - "to follow up after our interview."
    - "to ask about..."
    - "To say..."
- "Please let me know whether there is anything else I can provide for you"
- "One thing I wanted to clarify is ..."
- "Following up on..."
- "Please do not hesitate to ..."
    - "ask me any other questions you may have about ..."
    - "let me know if you need anything else from me."

Accepting or rejecting a job offer

Accepting a job offer

Congratulations! You got the job. Now, take a deep breath because the hard part is over. Once you have an offer on the table, there's not too much you can do to mess it up. They've made it clear that they want you and they will work hard to make it easy for you to transition into their company.

If you're ready to accept the offer as it is presented, you can prepare to write an email saying so.

To start, make sure the subject line of the email is clear. The company should have no doubts of what they will find when they open the email. You can say "[your name] - accepting job offer" or "Accepting job offer for [position name]"

As with all professional emails, you should address the specific person who sent you the job offer. Often, someone will call you on the phone before you receive the official offer to tell you they are extending an offer. This is the person you will likely address.

When you start your email, remember that the most important information always comes first. Don't bury the lede. Your first line should make it clear you are accepting the offer. Here are some examples:

"Please allow me to formally accept your job offer for full stack developer at ABC Gaming."
"It is my pleasure to accept your job offer for the community manager position as we discussed on the phone."
"I am happy to accept the accountant job offer at EZ Accounting Inc."

Next, don't forget to thank the company again for the opportunity. You were chosen out of possibly dozens of other candidates, and it is a privilege to be accepted for this position. You should also show your excitement to work for this company. You can say:

"Thank you very much for this opportunity and I look forward to applying my skills in this position."
"I am grateful for your offer and I look forward to working hard to help EZ Accounting grow."

After this, it's a good idea to restate the terms of the offer letter, including the salary, benefits and start date. This lets the company know that you have read the offer and agree with the offer as it is. In other words, there will be no doubt that you are ready to start working and are not looking to negotiate.

"As discussed, the starting salary will be $60,000 USD with benefits available after September 1, 2020. My first day will be May 15th."
"As the offer states, my salary will start at $72,000 USD and include the benefits package we discussed. I look forward to starting on Monday, January 12th."

You also want to include a paragraph asking whether there is anything you need to provide before your first day or bring on the start date.

"Please do not hesitate to contact me if there is anything you need before that day. You can reach me at this email address or on my cell phone: +1 210-555-1376."
"If there's anything else you need from me before my first day, please contact me at this email address or at 310 555 2871."

Finally, it doesn't hurt to add one more thank you as a polite and formal ending to your email. It may seem like a lot, but this is the common etiquette used in formal emails.

"Thank you again for giving me this opportunity to work for EZ Accounting."
"Once again, thank you for extending this opportunity and I look forward to be a part of your team."

Above all, be polite and professional. You will get to know your new co-workers on a personal level soon, but, for now, keep your communication formal.

Rejecting an offer

Sometimes, you might get an offer and realize that the position simply isn't for you. Maybe you decide to take another opportunity or just remain in your current company. Now, you have to send an email or make a call to reject the offer.

The most important thing when rejecting an opportunity is to avoid ruining the relationship and closing possible opportunities for the future. You may not be ready for this job right now, but you never know if you will want to work there in the future. Furthermore, most industries are smaller than you think. Being rude to one person in your industry could affect your opportunities at other companies. People talk, and being polite is important. Always.

Also, make sure you are clear about why you are rejecting the offer. At this point, the company has spent a lot of time interviewing you, and it's fair that they know why you have chosen not to work for them.

Finally, be prompt with your response.[7] Consider that the company has a need to fill this position, and if you choose not to accept, they need to start considering their other choices.

You may want to consider making a phone call to reject an offer, especially if you spent a lot of time speaking with one recruiter or hiring manager throughout the interview process. This is the best way to maintain a good relationship and show your respect.

If you do choose to send an email, here's how it may look:

Dear Anthony,
Thank you so much for offering me the project leader position at NIO

Pharmaceuticals.
After careful thought, I have decided to accept a position at another company. Therefore, I must turn down your offer.
Thank you for taking the time to speak with me and I truly hope we meet again in the future.
Respectfully,
Sally Michaels

This email can be brief. There is no need for a long explanation. Hiring managers know that the job market is competitive and not everyone will accept their offer. Most of all, be polite and clear, and everything will be okay.

Useful phrases:

- "Thank you so much for …"
- "I'm very grateful for …"
- "I appreciate your offer of …"
- "After careful thought …"
- "After much consideration …"
- "Having considered carefully …"
- "While this position is a great opportunity …"
- "Thank you once again for …"
- "I really enjoyed getting to know the team …"
- "I appreciate the time you spent with me …"

Reasons to reject an offer:

- "I've decided to accept a position at another company."
- "I've realized I'm not ready to leave my current position at the moment."
- "Your offer is not quite the right fit for my professional goals right now."
- "I've decided to pursue a position that will allow me to focus more on [skill/field]."
- "I don't believe I'm ready for the position you are offering me at this time."

Rejection: Recognizing things out of your control

Being rejected hurts.

Especially when you are very interested in a position and a company, it's natural to feel like you did something wrong or you were not good enough. But this isn't always the case.

Remember, corporate job openings can receive about 250 applications for a single position.[8] Just by making it to the interview stage, you already passed the large majority of these applicants.

But even if you follow all the advice in this book and do everything perfectly, sometimes you still get rejected. In these situations, it's important to recognize that some things are out of your control. There are dozens of reasons you were not the one chosen this time.

Sometimes the company decides to hire someone internally or to postpone hiring someone altogether. The company may choose someone who has a little more experience than you or fits the company culture a little better. And these are just the professional reasons.

When there are two or more qualified, experienced candidates at the end of the process, the final decision can be based on the smallest things. For instance, another candidate may have been a little funnier in their interview, or someone else had a little more in common with their interviewer.[9]

The point is, being rejected after an interview does not mean you did something wrong. It does not mean you were an unqualified candidate. And being rejected definitely should not stop you from trying again.

Being rejected is, most importantly, an opportunity to learn and grow. When you receive the rejection call or email, your response will determine whether the company will consider you in the future.

When you respond, remember to thank the interviewers for their time and the opportunity. Then, ask them what you can do better for the next time and how you can hear about more job openings. In other words, build a relationship, and show you are still intent on working for their company or in the same industry.

You can even ask whether your English level was a consideration in the decision. Whatever the answer, you should leave the conversation with a clear idea of what you can learn and improve upon to be more competitive when the next opportunity arrives.

Why you should act now

I have a client from Brazil who wanted to change her job. She didn't really use English at work, but she wanted to move to an international company, possibly outside of Brazil. She was practicing her English communication skills with me for when this day came. I mentioned she should start practicing for interviews, but she decided to wait. She wasn't concerned yet because she hadn't really started looking yet. This change wasn't an immediate priority for her.

One day, without warning, a recruiter called. She talked with him once or twice and suddenly had an interview scheduled for the next week.

In today's business environment, your next interview could come at any moment. With the competitive job market and social networks like LinkedIn, recruiters are always looking for top talent to speak with and bring to their clients.

Maybe you don't have an interview in English in the near future. Perhaps you are comfortable in your current job and think this is a skill you will never need. But with the rise of English as the language for international business, there is no denying this is a useful skill to have. It doesn't matter whether you have an interview tomorrow or will not have one for several years. The time to prepare yourself is now.

Interviewing is a skill. It's something some people are naturally good at, and others are not. Even if the interview is in your native language, it is something you will practice. Fortunately, it is something you can strengthen before you have to apply the skill.

As with any skill, it's better to learn before you need to apply it. Most people learn how to build a house before they begin building a house.

Similarly, like other skills, you will learn when you start doing interviews. You will learn by doing. Your first house will not be perfect, but they will get better with each one you build.

This means that it is crucial to practice with every opportunity you have. If you do not get a job offer the first time you interview, do not be discouraged from taking the next chance.

It also means that you should start applying what you learn now. Don't just read this book, try it yourself. Apply the tips and advice and speak to a friend or make a recording of yourself. You can read all the right answers and tips and tricks, but unless you practice your answers, you won't be ready when that recruiter calls. Don't be caught unprepared.

Glossary of terms

Hard skills or technical skills – abilities that are easy to quantify and that you can develop. These include typing speed, language proficiency, using specific software

Soft skills (also called "people skills" or "interpersonal skills") – abilities related to the way you interact with others and are harder to objectively judge. These include patience, communication, flexibility, time management

Behavioral Interview – an interviewing technique where the candidate is asked to describe a past behavior to determine their suitability for the position. Behavioral questions often begin with "Tell me about a time…"

STAR Method – An interview technique used to help organize stories. STAR stands for "Situation, Task, Action, Result"

CAR Method – "Context, Action, Result" The CAR method is another technique to answer behavioral interview questions and help organize stories

Human resources (HR) – The department of a company responsible for managing the people in that company. The HR department is responsible for hiring, interviewing, training and managing employees

CEO – Chief Executive Officer. The leader and main decision maker in a company

Candidate – A person being considered for a vacant job position

Small talk – Polite conversation usually at the beginning of an interaction. It usually involves topics unrelated to the purpose of the meeting such as the weather, family or travel

Resume – A document created to show the background, experience and skills of a person. They are typically created for vacant job positions. Resumes should be customized for each application

CV – Curriculum Vitae (Latin for "Course of Life") A written chronological record of someone's work experience and education. Not usually made specifically for one position

Notes

[1] Pareles, Jon, and Adam Nagourney. "Whitney Houston, Pop Star Whose Voice Was a Clarion Call, Dies at 48." Https://Nytimes.com, 13 Feb. 2012, archive.nytimes.com/query.nytimes.com/gst/fullpage-9C02E4DA153CF930A25751C0A9649D8B63.html.

[2] Zhang, L. (2019, October 14). The Interview Technique You Should Be Using. Retrieved May 3, 2020, from https://www.themuse.com/advice/the-interview-technique-you-should-be-using

[3] Hall, K. (2019). Stories that stick: how storytelling can captivate customers, influence audiences, and transform your business. Retrieved from https://www.amazon.com/Stories-That-Stick-Storytelling-Captivate-ebook/dp/B07KF2328Z

[4] Doyle, A. (2020, January 19). What Is Company Culture? Retrieved May 3, 2020, from https://www.thebalancecareers.com/what-is-company-culture-2062000

[5] Workopolis. (2015, June 16). Study: How quickly do interviewers really make decisions? Retrieved from https://careers.workopolis.com/advice/study-how-quickly-do-interviewers-really-make-decisions/

[6] Skillings, P. (2020, March 25). Top 12 Best Questions to Ask at the End of the Job Interview. Retrieved May 3, 2020, from https://biginterview.com/best-questions-to-ask-end-interview/

[7] Larssen, A. G. (2019, December 15). How to Gracefully Turn Down a Job Offer. Retrieved May 3, 2020, from https://www.themuse.com/advice/how-to-gracefully-turn-down-a-job-offer

[8] Sullivan, J. (2015, July 23). Why You Can't Get A

Job ... Recruiting Explained By the Numbers. Retrieved May 3, 2020, from https://www.ere.net/why-you-cant-get-a-job-recruiting-explained-by-the-numbers/

[9] Workopolis. (2013, August 28). Who gets hired: Why employers select one candidate over another. Retrieved May 3, 2020, from https://careers.workopolis.com/advice/who-gets-hired-why-employers-select-one-candidate-over-another/

About the Author

James is a communications coach who helps non-native English speakers advance in their careers using English. He is passionate about motivating clients from all over the world to thrive in today's English-speaking business world. James is an avid traveler and has visited more than 40 countries. He currently lives in Armenia, Colombia with his partner. This is his first book.

You can learn more about James and his services at https://englisharrow.com/about/

www.ingramcontent.com/pod-product-compliance
Lightning Source LLC
Chambersburg PA
CBHW070254220526
45465CB00004B/1621